Welcome to Somalia

By Elma Schemenauer

The Child's World®

Welcome to the WORLD

Published by The Child's World®
1980 Lookout Drive
Mankato, MN 56003-1705
800-599-READ
www.childsworld.com

Content Adviser: Dr. Charles Gichana Manyara, Associate Professor, Department of
Geography, Radford University, Radford, Virginia.
Design and Production: The Creative Spark, San Juan, Capistrano, CA
Editorial: Publisher's Diner, Wendy Mead, Greenwich, CT
Photo Research: Deborah Goodsite, Califon, NJ

Special thanks to Daniel Berendes and Nimco Duale for their assistance with this book.

Cover and title page photo: Liba Taylor/Panos Pictures
Interior Photos: Alamy: 20 (Mark Pearson), 22, 30 (Liba Taylor), 31 (Steve Morgan/
Photofusion Picture Library); AP Photo: 3 top, 19 (Jean-Marc Bouju), 3 bottom, 21
(Elizabeth A. Kennedy), 26 (Sayyid Azim); Corbis: 6, 8 (Yann Arthus-Bertrand), 10 (Bettmann),
18, 23, 24 (Kevin Fleming); Getty Images: 7 (Stephen Morrison/AFP), 15 (Andrea Booher/
Photographer's Choice), 17 (Mike Goldwater/Christian Aid/Exclusive), 29 (Khamis Ramadhan/
Panapress); iStockphoto.com: 3 middle, 9 (Vera Bogaerts), 28 (Ufuk Zivana); Landov: 13
(Antony Njuguna/Reuters), 14 (Grant Fleming/Reuters), 27 (Xinhua); Lonely Planet Images:
11 (Jean-Bernard Carillet); NASA Earth Observatory: 4 (Reto Stockli); Panos Pictures: 25
(Giacomo Pirozzi); Peter Arnold, Inc.: 12 (Thielker/Ullstein); Photo Researchers, Inc.: 16
(Hubertus Kanus).
Map: XNR Productions: 5

Library of Congress Cataloging-in-Publication Data
Schemenauer, Elma.
  Welcome to Somalia / by Elma Schemenauer.
    p. cm. — (Welcome to the world)
  Includes index.
  ISBN 978-1-59296-976-0 (library bound : alk. paper)
  1. Somalia—Juvenile literature. I. Title.
  DT401.5.S345 2008
  967.73—dc22
                                    2007036353

Contents

Where Is Somalia? 4

The Land 6

Plants and Animals 8

Long Ago 11

Somalia Today 12

The People 14

City Life and Country Life 17

Schools and Language 18

Work 21

Food 22

Pastimes 25

Holidays 26

Fast Facts About Somalia 28

How Do You Say... 30

Glossary 31

Further Information 32

Index 32

Where Is Somalia?

If you were soaring high above Earth, you would see huge land areas with water around them. These land areas are called **continents.** Somalia is the easternmost country on the continent of Africa. Somalia forms a large part of the "Horn of Africa," an area that juts out into the water like the horn of a rhinoceros.

This picture gives us a flat look at Earth. Somalia is inside the red circle.

The Gulf of Aden lies to the north of Somalia. The Indian Ocean lies to the east. The three countries bordering Somalia are Djibouti (jeh-BOO-tee) to the northwest, Ethiopia to the west, and Kenya to the southwest.

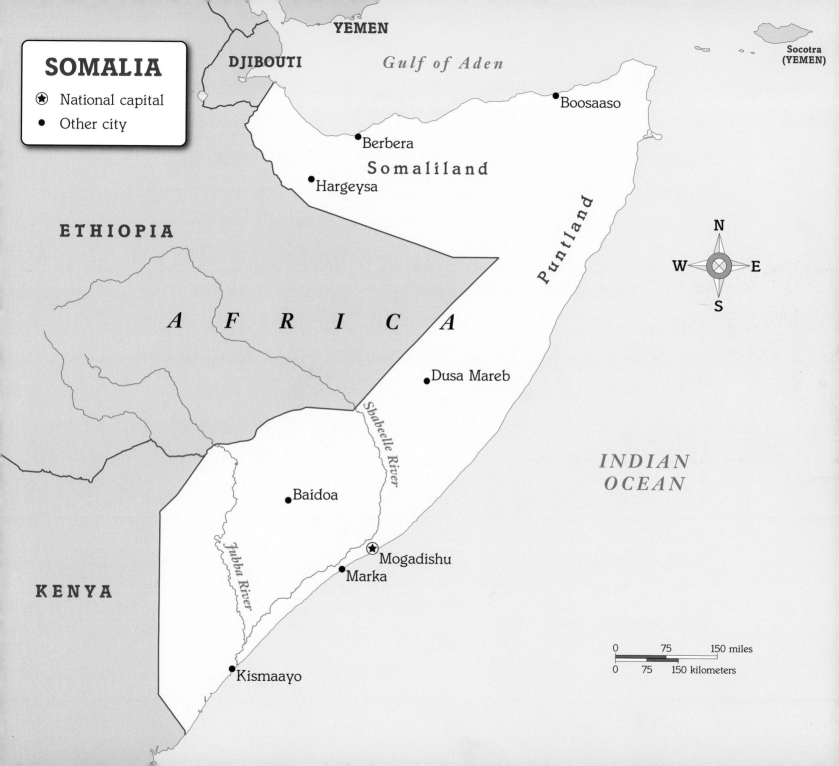

SOMALIA

★ National capital
● Other city

YEMEN

DJIBOUTI

Gulf of Aden

Socotra
(YEMEN)

● Boosaaso

● Berbera

S o m a l i l a n d

● Hargeysa

ETHIOPIA

Puntland

A F R I C A

● Dusa Mareb

Shabeelle River

● Baidoa

Jubba River

INDIAN
OCEAN

★ Mogadishu

● Marka

KENYA

● Kismaayo

N
W E
S

| 0 | 75 | 150 miles |
| 0 | 75 | 150 kilometers |

The Land

Most of Somalia is made up of flat or rolling plains. The northern portion of the country has a narrow coastal plain with mountain ranges behind it. Somalia's southern part has two main rivers, the Jubba and the Shabeelle. They flow toward the Indian Ocean.

A dry riverbed in Somalia

During the main rainy season, a river may overflow its banks.

Somalia has four seasons. It has two dry seasons and two wet seasons. The first dry season is from December to March. April to June is the main rainy season, when grasses and flowers burst out almost everywhere—even in the deserts. Then Somalia has its second dry season from July to September. The country has only light rains from October to November. Even with its two rainy seasons, Somalia is a hot, dry country.

Plants and Animals

During much of the year, scattered grasses and bushes, including thorn bushes, struggle to grow on Somalia's dry plains. The plains near the Jubba and Shabeelle Rivers get a bit more rain, so the trees, bushes, and grasses grow thicker and taller there. In the northern mountains, where it is a bit cooler, some forests of junipers and other trees grow.

These shrubs are some of the only plants that can survive in Somalia's dry climate.

Some zebras like to live in open spaces, such as grasslands.

Somalia's animals include badgers, jackals, gazelles, and antelopes. There are also a few elephants, giraffes, and zebras. Among Somalia's big cats are lions and leopards. Birds include eagles, vultures, doves, and ostriches. In Somalia, people need to watch out for poisonous snakes! These dangerous snakes include cobras, puff adders, and mambas.

Did you know?

Somali teenage boys often herd their families' camels, moving them from place to place in search of water and pasture. During this time the boys' only food is camels' milk. Sometimes a hungry young camel herder will drink 6 to 10 quarts of milk a day.

Troops from Italy landing on the shore of North Somalia

Long Ago

A painting made by some of the ancient people of Somalia.

Long ago, groups of people from several parts of Africa moved into the area now called Somalia. Arabs also arrived from Asia, bringing a religion called **Islam** with them. By about the year 1100, the whole area was Islamic. People raised animals, farmed, and traded. **Clans,** or groups of related families, sometimes fought over the right to use water and pasture land.

In the 1800s, Europeans arrived. Britain set up bases in what is now northern Somalia. In return for the Somali chiefs' trade and cooperation, Britain agreed to protect them from enemy clans. South of the British bases, Italy set up bases of its own. In time, Britain and Italy began governing the area.

In 1960, Somalis started running their own government. The British and Italian regions joined to form one new country, Somalia.

Somalia Today

Several years after the new country of Somalia was formed, fighting among clans got worse. Some clans fought the government. In 1991, a group of clans drove out President Mohammed Siad Barre, and the government fell apart.

The next year was very dry, so Somalia's people could not raise much food. Many people starved to death. The United Nations sent food as well as soldiers to make peace among the warring clans. But the clans fought over the food and drove out the soldiers. The last United Nations soldiers left in 1995. In 2000, a new temporary Somali government was set up. Four years later, new leaders took office.

A young child waves to troops from the United Nations.

Unfortunately, the new government has faced many challenges. There have been problems with some clan leaders and nearby Ethiopia. Two northern areas called Somaliland

Somali president Abdulahi Yusuf (left) celebrates his election with his prime minister Mohammed Ali Ghedi in 2004.

and Puntland have set up their own governments. In 2006, rebel forces fought against the government and took over some areas. Despite these conflicts, many people hope the new government will bring peace and order to Somalia's war torn land.

Did you know?

The United Nations is an international organization that provides aid to countries and tries to end conflicts within and between countries. It also supports environmental and social programs.

13

The People

The tall, slim people who make up most of Somalia's population are called Somalis. Somalis believe that they are all related, even though they are divided into several clans. Some think they came from southern Ethiopia. Others

A group of Somalis listen to news from a radio in Dusa Mareb.

think they all descended from one Arab father and one African mother.

It is hard to be certain what happened long ago, but Somalis all share the same culture and language. Parts of their culture and language are Arabic. Other parts are African. Besides Somalis, the country also has small numbers of Italians, Arabs, Pakistanis, and Indians.

Most of the people living in the country are Somali.

Mogadishu is the capital of Somalia.

City Life and Country Life

A shepherd watches over goats and sheep by a river.

Fewer than one-third of Somalia's people live in towns or cities. Many town and city dwellers live in rectangular houses with flat roofs. In big cities, such as Mogadishu and Kismaayo, there are hotels, banks, restaurants, and post offices just like those in the United States.

Many country people are **nomads** who move around to find water and pasture for their animals. Their round huts have **thatched** roofs, and walls covered with mats or animal hides. When it is time to move, the nomads take their homes apart and load them onto their camels' backs.

Did you know?

Though Somalia has no railroads, it does have some gravel and dirt roads. There is only one paved road. It runs from the port of Berbera in the northwest down to Mogadishu, and then south to Kismaayo.

17

Children go to a temporary school after leaving their homes because of clan fighting.

Schools and Language

The Somali government used to run free schools for children ages 6 through 14. After the government fell apart in 1991, many of its schools closed.

Today some schools are open. Many are **Koranic schools.** In these schools, children study the Koran (the holy book of Islam), which is written in Arabic. Some areas also have schools that are paid for by Somalis or by people from other countries who are trying to help. In the cities, wealthy families hire **tutors,** or private teachers.

Did you **know?**

People used to write the Somali language using several different alphabets. In 1973 the government decided that Somali should be written in letters like those we use for English.

18

Young girls listen to their teacher at a school in Hargeysa.

Somali became Somalia's official national language in 1973. It's an African-Asian language. Among other languages spoken in Somalia are Arabic, Italian, English, and Swahili.

19

A woman tends to crops near the lower end of the Shabeelle River.

Work

A woman runs her own cloth shop in a marketplace.

Sixty percent of Somalis are nomads who herd goats, sheep, camels, and cattle. Another 25 percent of the Somali people are farmers. They grow bananas, sugarcane, cotton, mangoes, corn, sesame seeds, and a cornlike plant called **sorghum.** Some Somalis also fish or do other types of work.

Somalia is a dry country with very few natural resources, so Somalis find it hard to make a living. Clan wars have made it even harder, especially since the government fell apart in 1991. Even with its current government, the country has torn been apart by fighting. Despite Somalia's problems, some people have been able to operate some businesses.

A mother and daughter make pasta together.

Food

For breakfast a Somali family might have rolls or flat bread with tea, or perhaps liver and onions. At noon they might eat rice or pasta with sauce, and perhaps goat or camel meat.

The evening meal is light— often flat bread or rice with salad. Somalis like milk, but they prefer milk from goats or camels rather than from cows. Other favorite drinks are coffee and tea with lots of sugar. It is against the Islamic religion to drink wine or other alcoholic drinks, or to eat pork.

Hunger is still a problem in Somalia. Other countries send food, but clan wars often keep it from getting to the hungry. Life is a little better in Somaliland and Puntland, but food is still scarce.

A woman cooks on an open fire using a clay pot.

A group of Somalis gather to sing.

Pastimes

Somalia is a land of poets. Somalis make up poems about God, daily life, camels, love, peace, and war. They recite their poems at events such as feasts, weddings, or blessings of new babies. They even hold contests in which poets compete

Creating stories and poems are an important part of Somali culture.

to see who is the best. Somalis also enjoy music, dancing, plays, and storytelling. Some stories are about animals, and others are about long ago heroes.

Holidays

Somali Muslims read the Koran.

Among the yearly holidays are New Year's Day on January 1, Labor Day on May 1, and Foundation of the Republic Day on July 1. During the month of Ramadan, followers of Islam go without food from sunrise to sunset each day.

The holiday of Eid al Adha celebrates the **prophet** Abraham's strong faith in God. Children love Eid al Adha because stores sell special toys and candy, and there are amusement parks where the children can play.

Somalis face many problems, including hunger, lack of schooling, and fighting between different groups. Yet they have not given up, a Somali proverb says, "If people come together, they can even mend a crack in the sky." Somalis hope to work toward a better future, along with other people from around the world.

A group of children sing at a school celebration.

Fast Facts About Somalia

Area: 246,000 square miles (about 637,000 square kilometers)—a bit smaller than Texas

Population: About 9 million people

Capital City: Mogadishu

Other Important Cities: Berbera, Kismaayo, Marka, Boosaaso, Hargeysa, and Baidoa

Money: The Somali shilling

National Flag: The flag is light blue with a white, five pointed star in the middle. The blue stands for the United Nations, of which Somalia is a member. The white color stands for peace, and the star's five points stand for Somalia's five regions.

National Holiday: Foundation of the Somali Republic, July 1

National Language: Somali

Official Name: Somalia

Famous Somalis:

Abdirashid Ali Shermarke: former president

Iman: fashion model

Mohammed Abdullah: Somali leader who fought against British rule

Mohammed Ibrahim Warsame Hadrawi: poet

Mohammed Siad Barre: former president

National Song: *"Soomaaliya Toosoo"* ("Somalia Wake Up")

> Somalia wake up,
> Wake up and join hands together
> And we must help the weakest of our people
> All of the time.

Somali Folktale: The Ancient Land of Punt

In ancient times, there was a land called Punt. No one knows for certain where it was exactly. Some think what is now Somalia was a part of this area. This historic land was famous for its frankincense and myrrh. The ancient Egyptians visited the land of Punt many times to trade for these strong-smelling materials. Pictures of the people of Punt can be seen in the artwork of ancient Egyptians.

In Somalia today, the name of these ancient people lives on through a special region called Puntland.

How Do You Say...

ENGLISH	SOMALI	HOW TO SAY IT
hello	nabad miiya	na-bat MEE-ya
good-bye	nabad gelyo	na-bat GEL-yo
thank you	mahadsanid	mah-had-SAH-neet
one	kow	KOH
two	laba	LAH-bah
three	saddex	SAH-deh
Somalia	Soomaalia	so-MAW-lee-a

Glossary

clans (KLANZ) Clans are large groups of families who consider themselves related. Clans are an important part of Somali culture.

continents (KON-tih-nents) Most of Earth's land lies in huge land areas called continents. Somalia is on the easternmost side of the continent of Africa.

Islam (IS-lahm) Islam is a set of beliefs about God (called Allah) and his prophet Muhammad. Many Somalis follow Islam.

Koranic schools (koh-RRAHN-ik SKOOLZ) In Koranic schools, people study the book of Islam, called the Koran. Some Koranic schools still exist in Somalia.

nomads (NOH-madz) Nomads are people who move from place to place rather than living in one spot. Many people in Somalia's countryside are nomads.

prophet (PRAHF-et) A prophet is someone who speaks for God. The holiday of Eid al Adha celebrates the prophet Abraham's faith in God.

sorghum (SOR-gum) Sorghum is a tall plant with wide leaves that is grown in warm areas. Some Somali farmers grow sorghum, which is often used as food for farm animals.

thatched (THATCHD) Thatched roofs are made of carefully stacked grass or straw. Many homes in Somalia's countryside have thatched roofs.

tutors (TOO-terz) Tutors are teachers who work one on one with students instead of teaching an entire classroom of people. Some wealthy Somali children are taught by tutors.

Further Information

Read It

Fox, Mary Virginia. *Somalia*. New York: Children's Press, 1996.

Hamilton, Janice. *Somalia in Pictures*. Minneapolis, MN: Twenty-First Century Books, 2007.

Hoffman, Mary, and Karin Littlewood (illustrator). *The Color of Home*. New York: Phyllis Fogelman Books, 2002.

Moriarty, Kathleen, and Amin Amir (illustrator). *Wiil Waal: A Somali Folktale*. St. Paul, MN: Minnesota Humanities Commission, 2007.

Look It Up

Visit our Web page for lots of links about Somalia:
http://www.childsworld.com/links

Note to Parents, Teachers, and Librarians: We routinely verify our Web links to make sure they are safe, active sites—so encourage your readers to check them out!

Index

animals, 9
area, 28
capital city, 17, 28
education, 18
farming, 21
flag, 28
food, 20–21
government, 11, 12, 13
history, 11
holidays, 26
industries, 21
language, 18, 19
major cities, 17, 28
money, 28
national song, 29
natural resources, 6, 7
nomads, 17, 21
plants, 8
population, 28
Puntland, 13, 23
Somaliland, 13, 23